VERMONT

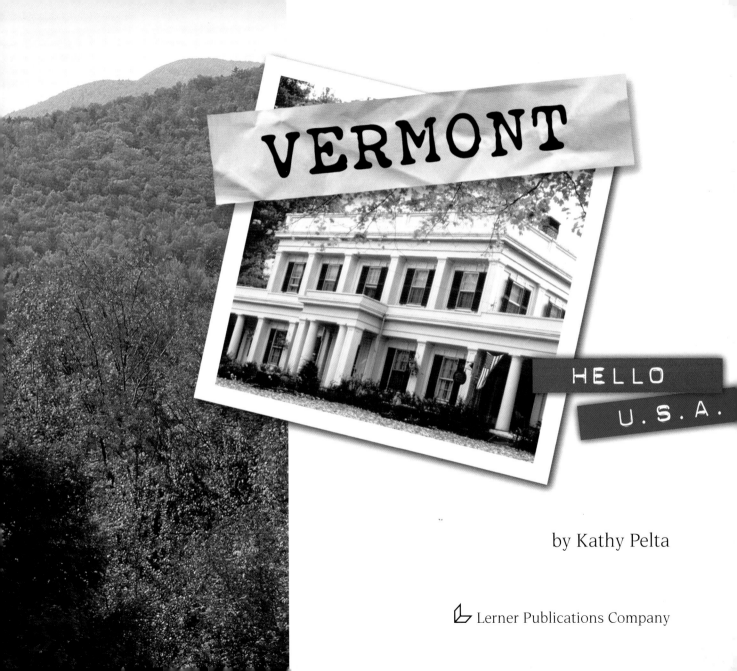

VERMONT

HELLO
U.S.A.

by Kathy Pelta

Lerner Publications Company

You'll find this picture of maple leaves at the beginning of every chapter in this book. Maple trees are important to Vermont's economy—the state produces more maple syrup than any other state. Vermonters make about 460,000 gallons of maple syrup each year. It takes about 40 gallons of sap from a maple tree to make 1 gallon of syrup.

Cover (left): A snow-covered bridge in Lake Champlain, Vermont, at the boundary between Vermont and New York. Cover (right): A selection of maple syrups and sugars from a Vermont-based company. Pages 2–3: Green Mountain National Forest near Rochester, Vermont. Page 3: The Arlington Inn in Arlington, Vermont.

This book is available in two editions:
Library binding by Lerner Publications Company, a division of Lerner Publishing Group
Soft cover by First Avenue Editions, an imprint of Lerner Publishing Group
241 First Avenue North
Minneapolis, MN 55401 U.S.A.

Website address: www.lernerbooks.com

Library of Congress Cataloging-in-Publication Data

Pelta, Kathy.
    Vermont / by Kathy Pelta (Rev. and expanded 2nd ed.)
      p. cm. — (Hello U.S.A.)
    Includes index.
    ISBN: 0–8225–4074–6 (lib. bdg. : alk. paper)
    ISBN: 0–8225–4135–1 (pbk. : alk. paper)
    1. Vermont—Juvenile literature. [1. Vermont.] I. Title. II. Series.
  F49.3 .P45 2002
  974.3—dc21   2001001742

Manufactured in the United States of America
1 2 3 4 5 6 – JR – 07 06 05 04 03 02

CONTENTS

In autumn, the Green Mountains are ablaze with colorful leaves.

THE LAND

Green Mountain State

The name Vermont comes from the French words *vert* (for "green") and *mont* (for "mountain"). Vermont's tree-covered ranges run north to south down the center of the small state, giving it the nickname the Green Mountain State.

At one time, Vermont's mountains were twice as high as they are in modern times. About 80,000 years ago, huge masses of ice called **glaciers** inched slowly across much of North America. The weight and force of the glaciers sculpted Vermont's peaks and carved its valleys. When the ice melted, it filled low areas, creating lakes and rivers.

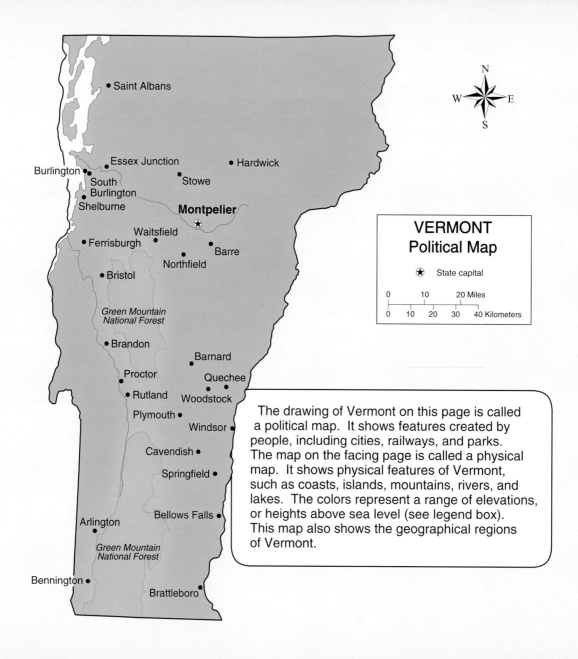

Saint Albans

N
W   E
S

Essex Junction   ● Hardwick
Burlington ●
  ● Stowe
South
Burlington
Shelburne
Montpelier
☆

Waitsfield
● Ferrisburgh
  ● Barre
Northfield

● Bristol

*Green Mountain
National Forest*

● Brandon

Barnard

Proctor
Quechee
● Rutland
Woodstock

Plymouth ●

Windsor ●

Cavendish ●

Springfield ●

Bellows Falls ●

Arlington ●

*Green Mountain
National Forest*

Bennington ●

Brattleboro ●

**VERMONT
Political Map**

☆   State capital

0   10   20 Miles
0   10   20   30   40 Kilometers

The drawing of Vermont on this page is called a political map. It shows features created by people, including cities, railways, and parks. The map on the facing page is called a physical map. It shows physical features of Vermont, such as coasts, islands, mountains, rivers, and lakes. The colors represent a range of elevations, or heights above sea level (see legend box). This map also shows the geographical regions of Vermont.

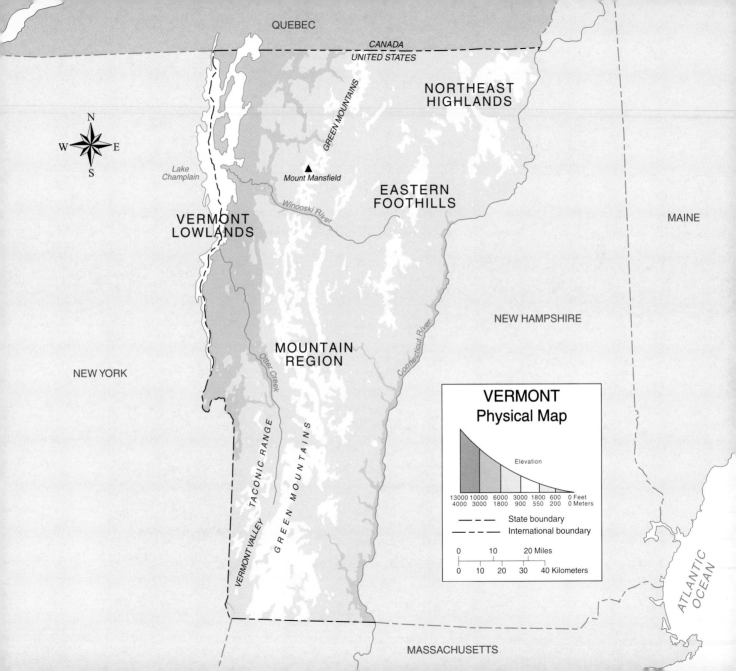

QUEBEC

CANADA
UNITED STATES

NORTHEAST
HIGHLANDS

N
W   E
S

Lake Champlain

GREEN MOUNTAINS

▲
Mount Mansfield

EASTERN
FOOTHILLS

Winooski River

VERMONT
LOWLANDS

MAINE

Connecticut River

NEW HAMPSHIRE

NEW YORK

MOUNTAIN
REGION

Otter Creek

TACONIC RANGE

VERMONT VALLEY

GREEN MOUNTAINS

VERMONT
Physical Map

Elevation

| 13000 | 10000 | 6000 | 3000 | 1800 | 600 | 0 Feet |
| 4000 | 3000 | 1800 | 900 | 550 | 200 | 0 Meters |

– – – State boundary

– – – International boundary

| 0 | 10 | | 20 Miles |
| 0 | 10 | 20 | 30 | 40 Kilometers |

ATLANTIC
OCEAN

MASSACHUSETTS

Vermont is part of New England, a region in the northeastern United States that once belonged to Britain. Vermont's northern neighbor is the Canadian province of Quebec. Massachusetts is to the south of Vermont. The long Connecticut River forms the boundary between Vermont and its eastern neighbor, New Hampshire. To the west is New York, with Lake Champlain marking part of the border.

Vermont's largest lake, Lake Champlain, marks the western border of the state.

Vermont has four land regions—the Northeast Highlands, the Eastern Foothills, the Mountain Region, and the Vermont Lowlands. Granite mountains and swiftly flowing streams cover the Northeast Highlands. In the thick forests, moose, white-tailed deer, and black bears roam. Sand and loose rock left by glaciers make the soil poor for farming. Logging is the region's main industry.

South and west of the Northeast Highlands are the rolling hills, valleys, and farms of the Eastern Foothills. In the valleys, farmers grow apple trees and raise dairy cattle. To the west, the foothills gradually rise to meet the ranges of the Mountain Region.

Black bears inhabit the Green Mountains.

Vermont's forests and mountains offer trails for hikers, such as Camel's Hump in the Green Mountains.

Two major mountain chains rise in the Mountain Region. The Green Mountains, called the backbone of Vermont, stretch the entire length of the region. Rabbits and foxes dart through the forests, which are also home to woodchucks, mink, and porcupines. Mount Mansfield, the highest point in the state, rises 4,393 feet in the Green Mountains.

The Taconic Range, also in the Mountain Region, extends along the state's western border. The long, narrow Vermont Valley separates the Taconics from the Green Mountains. Miners have dug **quarries,** or deep pits, to reach the large stores of limestone and marble that lie under the valley.

At its northern end, the Vermont Valley widens into the Vermont Lowlands, often called the Champlain Valley. Much of this region is sandwiched between Lake Champlain to the west and the Green Mountains to the east. Crops thrive in the fertile soil of the Vermont Lowlands. Burlington, the state's largest city, is located in this region.

Otter Creek, Vermont's longest river, flows north across the lowlands and empties into Lake Champlain. Several large rivers, including the Winooski, flow west into Lake Champlain from the Green Mountains. Other waterways run eastward from the Green Mountains and join the Connecticut River.

Vermont's summers are usually warm, with temperatures between 70° and 80° F. Summer thunderstorms can hit fast, pelting areas with rain and hail. The state's yearly **precipitation** (rain, snow, sleet, and hail) averages 39 inches. Around the middle of October, the first frost hardens the ground, and Vermont's oak and maple leaves turn brilliant shades of red and gold.

A vendor sells fresh produce at a farmer's market in Burlington.

Thousands of skiers visit Vermont each year to enjoy the snowy slopes.

Winters are long and harsh in Vermont, with an average temperature of 22° F. Heavy snow and ice blanket the state for months. The Vermont Lowlands receive about 60 inches of snow each year. Some places in the mountains get twice as much, attracting thousands of skiers.

The warm days of early spring bring out blossoms on fruit trees, and wildflowers brighten the land. Heavy rainstorms in the spring combine with melting snow to produce Vermont's "fifth season"— one of mud!

Vermont's mud season brings sloppy roads and trapped vehicles.

Although the mud season doesn't last long, mucky dirt roads often bring traffic to a standstill. Schools in the countryside sometimes close until the roads dry out.

In late spring, the landscape turns from brown to many shades of green, with grassy meadows, forests of evergreens, and newly leafed birch, maple, and beech trees. Residents call this time the greening of Vermont.

Wildflowers, such as these black-eyed Susans, bloom every spring throughout Vermont.

THE HISTORY

A Tradition of Independence

The first people to explore what later became Vermont were hunters who stalked their prey in mountains and forests thousands of years ago. By the year A.D. 1300, descendants of the early hunters had settled in valleys, where they grew crops. This Native American nation, called the Abenaki, lived in villages east of the lake they called Petoubouque. It was later named Lake Champlain.

The villagers arranged their daily tasks to fit the seasons. Spring was the time to plant beans, corn, and squash. Women and children gathered nuts and berries for food and medicine.

Corn was an important crop to the Abenaki Indians. They stored some of the crop in cellars for their winter food supply.

Abenaki Indians fished from the banks of Petoubouque Lake.

During warm weather, Abenaki families sometimes left their villages for weeks at a time to fish and hunt. They fished for salmon and trapped porcupines and squirrels. With bows and arrows, the hunters shot larger animals, such as moose and deer. Some Abenaki left home during the summer to exchange shells and arrowheads with members of nearby nations.

During the cold winters, villagers stayed close to home and survived on stored foods, such as corn and dried meat. The women sewed animal hides to make clothing and moccasins, while the men repaired tools and weapons.

The Abenaki got along with nearly all of their neighbors. But the Iroquois, who lived on the west side of Petoubouque Lake, were enemies of the Abenaki. For many years, these nations fought each other over territory.

In the spring, villagers planted corn *(above)* and boiled tree sap for syrup *(below).*

Samuel
de Champlain

In 1609 a French fur trader and explorer named Samuel de Champlain arrived in the area of Vermont. He had traveled by canoe from a settlement in Quebec, New France (later Canada). With him were two other Frenchmen and their Indian guides.

Near Petoubouque Lake, Champlain's group joined a raid against a band of Iroquois. The bows and arrows of the Iroquois were no match for Champlain's musket balls. The Frenchman shot two Iroquois leaders, causing the rest of the group to retreat. Later, the Abenaki persuaded Champlain to attack the Iroquois again. From then on, the Iroquois treated the French as their enemies, too.

When other French settlers reached the Champlain Valley, they put up forts to guard against Iroquois attacks. The first was Fort Sainte Anne, built in 1666 on an island in Lake Champlain.

Some of the French were traders who received furs from the Abenaki in exchange for wool blankets, metal pots, and guns. Along with the traders came **missionaries.** They taught the Abenaki about the Catholic religion and tried to make the Indians give up their traditional beliefs. Settlers disrupted the Abenaki way of life.

Without meaning to, the newcomers brought deadly germs. Unlike the Europeans, the Abenaki had never been exposed to smallpox, measles, cholera, and some other diseases. Nothing the Abenaki healers did could make their people well, and many of the Indians died.

Like the French, the British also had built settlements along the eastern seacoast of North America. Called **colonies,** these settlements included Massachusetts, New Hampshire, and New York, all of which surrounded the area of Vermont. But the British wanted more land. In the early 1700s, they tried to take areas that the French had claimed—but the French fought back.

The soft, warm fur of the beaver drew many hunters to Vermont. Beaver hides were sewn into fashionable hats, which sold in Europe for high prices.

During the French and Indian War, Indians in Vermont sided with the French.

The clashes between the British and French led to the French and Indian War (1754–1763). The British, with help from the Iroquois, raided French forts and destroyed Abenaki villages in the Champlain Valley. The French and the Abenaki attacked the British settlers in Massachusetts and New York.

Although the war was costly for the British, they defeated the French and the Abenaki. The British then took over most of New France, and settlers from the British colonies began to move into Abenaki territory in the Champlain Valley. Because the settlers invaded the Abenaki's hunting lands, the Indians could no longer provide for themselves as they once had. Most of them left the area.

At this time, both the New York and the New Hampshire colonies claimed the Abenaki homelands. New York's governor gave sections of the land to his friends. Conflicts arose when New Hampshire's governor granted some of the same land to his friends. This disputed territory became known as the New Hampshire Grants, or simply the Grants.

As more New Hampshire settlers moved into the Grants, New York complained to the British king. In 1764 the king declared that the land belonged to New York. The "Yorkers" then rushed to the Grants to demand rent from the New Hampshire settlers. Those who refused to pay were forced from their homes by Yorker sheriffs.

Some New Hampshirites staged a rebellion and asked a soldier named Ethan Allen for help. Allen and his friends formed a troop called the Green Mountain Boys. Their job was to protect the Grants from the Yorkers.

Fort Ticonderoga in Vermont was the site where Ethan Allen led the first colonial victory of the American Revolution.

Heroes or Outlaws?

Ethan Allen, leader of the Green Mountain Boys, was known for being bold and daring. Legends tell of Allen biting nails in two and knocking down an ox with one blow of his fist. But these stories were probably made up by the Green Mountain Boys. One thing is known for sure—Allen and his soldiers were brave enough to take on the Yorkers, who had more soldiers as well as the support of the British king.

Some people thought of Ethan Allen and the Green Mountain Boys as heroes, since the troop usually fought with their fists instead of with guns. But others saw them as bullies who refused to obey the law. The Green Mountain Boys roamed the Grants, stomping on the Yorkers' cornfields and burning their houses. The troop bullied Yorker officials by whipping them with sticks. Once, they put a Yorker in an armchair, lifted him up to a tavern sign, and left him there to dangle for two hours.

As punishment, Yorker officials threatened to hang any troop member who could be captured. But that didn't stop the Green Mountain Boys. The troop continued to protect their territory like fierce mountain lions. They even put a stuffed catamount (mountain lion) above the sign of their meeting place as a warning to all Yorkers. The snarling cat faced west, toward the colony of New York.

Ethan Allen and the
Green Mountain
Boys captured Fort
Ticonderoga in 1775.

Meanwhile, Britain demanded that the settlers pay high taxes. Britain also made new, stricter laws for all the colonies. As a result, many colonists refused to be loyal to the king any longer. By 1775 these events had led to the American Revolution—a war in which the colonies fought to gain their independence from Britain.

Soon after the war began, the Green Mountain Boys raided Britain's Fort Ticonderoga on the western shore of Lake Champlain. Taking the British guards by surprise, the soldiers were able to capture the fort without firing a shot.

General John Shark *(on horseback)* leads his colonial troops to the battle site at Bennington.

The Battle of Bennington

Two years into the American Revolution, the British army badly needed supplies, such as horses, wagons, weapons, and food. The army intended to restock in the town of Bennington, located in the Grants. Thinking that most of the Grants' residents were loyal to the British king, the soldiers planned to arrive in town and take the items they needed without trouble.

But when the colonists heard that the British soldiers were coming, they armed themselves for battle. Farmers and townspeople gathered alongside the Green Mountain Boys to keep horses and other supplies out of enemy hands. On the outskirts of Bennington, near the New York border, a troop of nearly 2,000 colonists awaited the British army's approach.

On August 16, 1777, the colonists fought against 1,000 British soldiers in the Battle of Bennington. With their victory, the colonists were able to prevent the British army from entering and taking control of what later became Vermont.

Although the Battle of Bennington was actually fought on New York soil, Vermonters take credit for its success. One of the world's largest battle monuments honors the Vermonters who defeated the British that summer day. Located in Bennington, Vermont, the Bennington Battle Monument stands 306 feet tall.

While the war raged, people in the Grants were planning for their future. In 1777 they set up their own independent government, adopted the name Vermont, and wrote a **constitution** (set of laws). Vermont's constitution outlawed slavery and gave all white men the right to vote—even men who were poor or did not own land.

The colonies defeated the British and in 1783 united to form a new country—the United States of America. Vermonters asked to be admitted to the Union, but Yorkers argued that they owned Vermont. To settle the dispute, Vermont paid New York $30,000 and in 1791 joined the Union as the 14th state.

During its first 10 years as part of the Union, Vermont was the fastest growing state in the nation. New settlers could purchase land at a fair price, and the population grew quickly. For the few remaining Abenaki, however, life was a struggle. Vermonters took over even more of the Abenaki's hunting land. Some of the Indians survived by selling goods to the settlers.

Settlers chopped down trees and burned them for heat and for cooking meals.

Like the Abenaki before them, Vermont's settlers lived by the seasons. They planted corn, beans, and squash in the spring and harvested in the fall. In the winter, they chopped firewood, made and repaired tools, and cut ice from frozen lakes. With the first spring thaw, they tapped maple trees for sweet sap, which they used to make syrup and candy.

To earn extra money, many Vermont farmers chopped down trees and burned them to make potash, a powdery ash used in soap and in fertilizer for crops. In those days, 2,000 pounds of wood was needed to make just 7 pounds of potash. By the early 1800s, Vermont's hills were nearly treeless.

On the bare hills, farmers planted apple orchards or raised wheat. But when other states began growing wheat, the competition hurt Vermont's farmers. Some of them left the state after a few dry summers parched their crops.

Hard times continued for Vermont when the United States and Britain went to battle in the War of 1812. At that time, the British navy controlled many shipping routes and would not let the United States deliver goods to France—Britain's enemy. But the United States depended on money earned from overseas trading and fought for the right to trade.

Many Vermonters did not support the war because it halted their trade with British-controlled Canada. Some residents turned to smuggling to get their goods across the Canadian border.

Vermont's trade centered around Lake Champlain. Workers floated logs down rivers to sawmills at the lake's edge. Farmers used the lake to transport their crops and cattle north to Canada. Canada, in turn, shipped goods Vermonters needed, including salt. By 1823 canals had been built, opening new water routes for shippers to haul goods from Lake Champlain south to New York City.

Rivermen guided logs to sawmills in rushing water.

Tools of the Trade

By the 1830s, Vermont's factories were buzzing. Workers used hand tools to pound and shape iron and other metals into everything from rifles to sewing machines to carriages. Factories began to look for ways to make their products more quickly. Before long, Vermonters had invented machine tools, which could drill, grind, cut, and press metal faster and more accurately than people could.

The small town of Windsor, Vermont, became a leader in the U.S. machine tool industry. By 1865 the Windsor Manufacturing Company was producing planers, lathes, punching presses, drills, and other machine tools. The firm later moved to Springfield, Vermont, where workers continued to invent and produce new tools.

Throughout most of the 1800s, Vermont's factory workers built machine tools that were considered the best in the world. As a result, Vermont's factories regularly supplied machine tools to large, out-of-state manufacturers. In this way, Vermont contributed to the growth of factories and businesses all across the nation.

THE WINDSOR MANUFACTURING CO.,
LATE E. G. LAMSON & CO.,
WINDSOR, VERMONT,
MANUFACTURERS OF MACHINISTS' TOOLS, MACHINERY FOR GUNS, PISTOLS, SEWING MACHINES
AND SEWING MACHINE NEEDLES,
Lamson's Patent Stone Channeling and Dressing Machines, Lane's Patent Circular Saw Mills, Ball's Patent Repeating and Single
Loading Rifles. The Lamson Converted Gun, (the only system of transform receiving Medal at the
World's Fair in Paris,) and Pomeroy's Patent Combination Screw and Griping Wrench.

THE LAMSON STONE CHANNELING MACHINE,
For Quarrying Marble, Slate, Sandstone and Gridstone rock; for Sinking Shafts in Mines and Tunnels, and for Grooving the smooth Pavements
of City Streets, belonging to the WINDSOR MANUFACTURING COMPANY, of Windsor, Vermont.

An advertisement for the Windsor Manufacturing Company features a worker operating the stone channeling machine.

Meanwhile, many sheep farmers in Champlain Valley grew rich by supplying the state's textile (cloth) mills with wool. But when farmers in the western United States and Australia also began producing wool, competition increased and prices dropped.

Vermont's dairy farmers often made their own butter, as this farm couple is doing.

During the late 1800s, **immigrants** from Ireland laid railroad tracks across Vermont. Trains began carrying the state's butter and cheese to Boston, New York, and other cities in nearby states. The trains also hauled slabs of granite, slate, and marble from Vermont to ports in other states for shipment overseas.

Because trains were able to carry Vermont's stone to many markets, the state's mining business grew. Companies hired marblecarvers from Italy, slateworkers from Wales, and stonecutters from Spain and Scotland. At the same time, immigrants from Hungary, Poland, Russia, and Canada arrived to work in Vermont's growing number of factories.

Trains also brought summer vacationers to Vermont. Hotels in the Green Mountains attracted city dwellers with advertisements praising the fresh mountain air and pure springwater. Tourism thrived in the early 1900s, but fewer people were moving to Vermont. For the first time, the state's population dropped.

Railroad construction jobs drew many Irish workers to Vermont.

At this time, about half of all working Vermonters had jobs in factories, mills, or quarries. Others worked in agriculture. Although dairy farms did well, some of Vermont's crop farmers could not make enough money and left to try farming in other states.

Vermonters faced other problems, too. In 1927 floods along the Winooski and Connecticut Rivers killed 85 people and destroyed homes, farms, bridges, and roads. Two years later, the state was hit by the Great Depression, a nationwide economic slump that lasted for about 10 years.

During the depression, factories closed in Vermont and across the country. Millions of people lost their jobs. The U.S. government hired some jobless Vermonters to work on flood-control projects, to pave roads, and to plant trees in the state.

When the Winooski River flooded in 1927, four people drowned on this street in Barre, Vermont.

Ski resorts have long been one of Vermont's leading tourist attractions.

The government workers also cut ski trails, and Vermont became a popular area for skiing, sledding, and ice-skating. In 1934 the state's first ski tow began operating on a farm in Woodstock, Vermont. Soon after, the first chairlift carried skiers up Mount Mansfield. Resorts in Vermont that once entertained only summer visitors now offered winter activities as well.

During World War II (1939–1945), 50,000 of Vermont's men and women served in the U.S. armed forces. Those at home also helped in the war effort. Granite workers used their skills to build chains for warship anchors. Women farmed or made machinery in factories. Children gathered milkweed pods to stuff life jackets and collected scrap paper, tin, copper, and brass for making war supplies.

In the years since World War II, Vermont has earned most of its money from manufacturing and tourism. But because Vermont does not have large cities, the state has a hard time attracting big companies. As a result, workers in Vermont tend to earn lower wages than workers in other parts of the country. So Vermonters are looking for ways to improve their state's economy.

During World War II, many Vermont women entered the workforce for the first time.

Some Vermonters hope to bring larger manufacturing companies into the state. Others would like to increase the number of small companies and encourage more tourism. Vermonters also struggle to balance their economic needs with the environment's survival. They must find ways to make money while preserving their state's natural beauty.

During the late 1990s, Vermont changed the way the state pays for schools. The state legislature passed Act 60, or the Equal Education Opportunity Act, a law that tries to make funding for schools more fair—students in all towns in Vermont, rich and poor, get the same amount of money from the state for their education. This way, Vermonters hope to make their state a place where everyone has a chance to thrive.

PEOPLE & ECONOMY

Villages and Vacationers

Many Vermonters live in small villages like this one.

Most of Vermont's early settlers lived in the countryside, far from their neighbors. Families had to rely on their own hard work to survive. Sometimes, though, friends got together for special tasks, such as husking corn, building barns, or making quilts.

In modern times, Vermonters are less isolated than the early settlers, but they are just as independent. About two-thirds of Vermont's residents still live in the countryside or in small towns tucked away in valleys or on hillsides.

A family carves pumpkins in Cavendish, Vermont.

With about 609,000 inhabitants, Vermont has fewer people than all the other states except Wyoming. Even Vermont's largest city, Burlington, has less than 40,000 people. The second largest city, Rutland, has half as many people as Burlington. Other cities include Barre, Bennington, Brattleboro, and Montpelier—the state capital.

Most Vermonters were born in the United States and have European backgrounds. About half are descendants of settlers from Britain and France. Others have German, Scottish, Polish, Swedish, or Dutch roots. African Americans and Native Americans have small populations in the state. Together they make up less than 1 percent of Vermont's residents. **Latinos** and Asian Americans each number about 1 percent of Vermont's population.

A farmer picks apples in rural Vermont.

About 2,000 Abenaki live in Vermont. To preserve the ways of their ancestors, Indians in the state hold special events, such as a fall harvest celebration. Some Abenaki teach their children the Abenaki language. Others visit schools to present information about Abenaki culture to young Vermonters.

A Vermont quilter proudly displays her craft.

Like the Abenaki, many other Vermonters practice skills passed on by their families. In fact, Vermont is known for its artists and craftspeople, who hold workshops to teach others their skills. Quilters, weavers, painters, sculptors, and potters sell their work at craft centers throughout the state.

In many villages and towns, well-kept old buildings give Vermont the look and feel of an earlier time. Artist Norman Rockwell captured this old-time look

Main Street in Hardwick, Vermont, is lined with charming old-fashioned buildings.

on covers he painted for a magazine called the *Saturday Evening Post.* Rockwell lived in Arlington, Vermont, for several years and used the town and its people as his models.

Inside sugarhouses, farmers boil sap to make syrup. About 40 gallons of sap make 1 gallon of maple syrup.

Vermont has many different museums devoted to showing the state's history. Exhibits feature everything from old machine tools to farm life in the 1700s to modern dairying. Some museums offer a firsthand look at workers on the job—cutting granite, carving marble, or making cheese, ice cream, or apple cider. At sugaring time, visitors at Vermont's sugarhouses can watch as guides collect sap from maple trees and boil it to make maple syrup.

The Bennington Museum, in Bennington, displays the works of one of the town's most famous residents—Anna Mary Robertson Moses, better known as Grandma Moses. This self-taught artist started painting at the age of 76. She continued to paint scenes of New England country life until her death at the age of 101.

The original steamship *Ticonderoga,* built in 1906, is open to tourists in Shelburne.

In Shelburne, Vermont, a reconstruction of an early American settlement shows visitors how the colonists lived. The Shelburne Museum features 37 buildings from the 1700s, including houses, a country store, a lighthouse, and a huge paddle-wheel boat that once steamed around Lake Champlain. Printers, weavers, basketmakers, and other craftspeople at the museum demonstrate their talents and hold workshops for visitors.

Vermont's hills ring with the sounds of music during outdoor summer concerts. Fairs and special events celebrate traditional music with fiddlers and banjo-pickers who play folk tunes that the early settlers once played.

Vermont's great outdoors attracts many people. Both residents and out-of-state visitors enjoy biking Vermont's peaceful back roads and climbing its mountains. Hikers follow a variety of trails, including abandoned rail beds and old logging roads. The

Folk musicians perform at many music festivals in Vermont.

Vermont's lakes offer many opportunities for water sports.

most famous footpath is the Long Trail, which winds along the peaks of the Green Mountains from Massachusetts, through Vermont, and up to Canada.

The state's fast-running rivers provide white-water rafters with an adventure. Vermont's lakes and rivers offer sailing and fishing. On Lake Champlain, scuba divers can explore old sunken ships!

Ever since the first vacationers came to Vermont in the mid-1800s, visitors have flocked to the state to ski and to admire the scenery. Thousands of service workers help these visitors enjoy their stay. Service workers assist people at motels and ski resorts, serve meals at restaurants, and pump gas at service stations.

A Fourth of July fireworks display cheers vacationers and locals at a Vermont harbor.

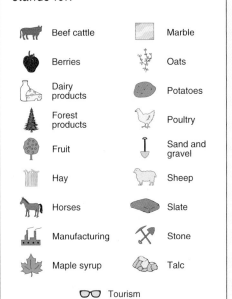

VERMONT
Economic Map

The symbols on this map show where different economic activities take place in Vermont. The legend below explains what each symbol stands for.

Beef cattle		Marble
Berries		Oats
Dairy products		Potatoes
Forest products		Poultry
Fruit		Sand and gravel
Hay		Sheep
Horses		Slate
Manufacturing		Stone
Maple syrup		Talc
	Tourism	

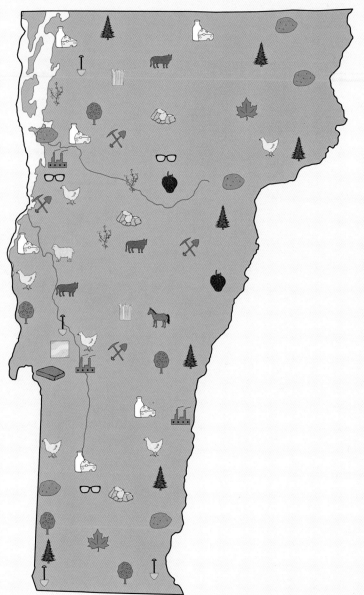

Vermont's quarries
supply granite
and marble.

Other Vermonters with service jobs include salesclerks, bank tellers, and doctors. Altogether, almost two out of three Vermonters have service jobs. Vermont's government workers do their jobs in places like public schools and hospitals. About 13 percent of Vermonters work for the government.

Dairy cows play an important role in Vermont agriculture.

Fewer than one out of every eight Vermonters work in manufacturing, though factories account for much of the state's earnings. At plants around Burlington, workers produce computers and computer software. Manufactured items in other parts of the state include granite monuments, teddy bears, flashlights, dishes, glassware, tools, clothing, guns, and furniture.

Although farms cover more than one-fifth of the state's land, only about 1 out of 25 people work in agriculture. Dairy farms supply milk and cream to Vermont's cheese-makers as well as to Boston and southeastern New England. Cheddar cheese, apples, and apple cider are important farm products, and most of the country's maple syrup comes from Vermont.

THE ENVIRONMENT

Protecting the Land

Vermonters are proud of the rustic beauty of their state—its winding roads, covered bridges, tiny villages, and hillside farms. Vermont's picture-postcard charm is the reason many residents choose to live there.

Natural beauty also makes the state attractive to visitors. Every year thousands of out-of-state vacationers travel to Vermont. These visitors need places to eat and sleep and safe roads on which to drive.

Some tourists enjoy the state so much they buy vacation homes in Vermont. Year-round residents also expect well-kept roads and want comfortable homes.

Opposite page: Vermont's countryside boasts more than 100 covered bridges.

Summer cottages are popular in Vermont.

To meet the needs of residents and vacationers, land developers buy land on which to build homes and to cut ski trails. But some Vermonters question how much land should be used in this way. Too much development can harm the environment.

Some Vermonters fear, for example, that cutting down trees to make ski trails on mountains will cause soil **erosion.** This wearing away of the earth's surface happens mostly in spring and summer, when rain and melting snow carry away soil. When the trees still stood, their roots helped hold the soil in place.

Some Vermonters also worry that building many houses close together will cause too much wear and tear on existing roads. And building more roads can disturb wildlife habitats and loosen the soil, causing more erosion.

Because of these concerns, Vermont has passed strict environmental laws. The laws allow some development to take place, but they also protect Vermont's natural beauty.

One law makes it difficult to subdivide large pieces of land. This means owners must get permission to break the land into smaller lots to sell to individual buyers. The subdividing might lead to overdevelopment if these buyers were to build homes on the small lots.

Many animals lose their homes when workers cut ski trails on Vermont's mountains.

Protecting Black Bears

When you think of a bear, you might imagine a strong, wild animal that is dangerous to humans. But people are actually more of a threat to bears. In Vermont, black bears are found in forests and mountains, where they live undisturbed by people. Experts fear that the state's black bears might lose their habitats (homes) to land developers.

Black bears need a lot of space in which to live and search for food. Roaming miles and miles each day, they nibble on nuts, berries, and insects. Black bears also need plenty of drinking water and safe dens for sleeping. But when developers build houses, condominiums, or roads in bear habitats, the bears have trouble finding food and shelter.

To discover exactly where black bears live and wander, experts look for the signs that bears leave behind. Sometimes researchers find teeth marks on tree trunks. Other times, they discover claw marks on a "baby-sitter tree," where a mother bear leaves her cubs for safety while she hunts. These clues about bear habitats help officials identify areas to protect from development.

Studying bear habitats is the first step in protecting Vermont's black bears. Experts are also working hard to educate land developers and residents about bear habitats. With these efforts, Vermonters hope to ensure a safe future for the state's black bears.

Vermont's environmental laws protect towns from overdevelopment, too. Developers must build in places that have a plentiful supply of water and a safe way to get rid of waste. And the new development cannot bring more people or traffic to an area than the community can handle.

The laws also protect scenic roads, waterways, and other features of Vermont's landscape. But not everyone agrees on which areas should be protected. What is important to one person—a stretch of woods or a winding creek—might not be to another.

Big billboards that hide the state's scenery are against the law in Vermont. Small wooden signs point the way instead.

For example, the laws that control development have caused problems for some of Vermont's farmers. Many owners of small farms have a hard time making a good living. The cost of running a farm is high, and some farmers cannot make enough money to pay all of their bills. These farmers want to make a profit by selling their land to developers.

Vermonters are proud of the beauty of their state and strive to protect it.

Before Vermont's environmental laws were passed, selling farmland to developers was fairly easy. But now, with so many limits in place, developers are much less likely to buy land from a farmer than before the laws were passed.

With the new laws, farmers are wondering what to do. Those hoping to sell their land to developers are upset by the laws. But homeowners who do not want the areas around them developed further welcome the limits. As the discussion continues over how much development is good for Vermont, many Vermonters are working to preserve the state's rustic beauty for future generations to enjoy.

Fun Facts

In 1977 fourth graders from Barnard, Vermont, chose the honeybee as the state insect.

Vermont's marble has been used in many famous buildings, such as the Supreme Court in Washington, D.C. Some of Vermont's marble is ground up for use in paints, plastics, and even chewing gum.

The first globe in the United States was made in 1799 by Vermonter James Wilson. Other inventions from Vermont include the rubber eraser, the steel carpenter's square, and the platform scale.

Vermont marble is used in buildings, monuments, and memorials.

Vermont was the first state to outlaw slavery. The law was included in the state's constitution, which was signed on July 2, 1777.

With about two-thirds of Vermonters living in rural areas, the state has the lowest percentatge of urban residents in the United States.

Millions of years ago, reptiles known as plesiosaurs swam in Vermont's Lake Champlain. Some people say that Champ, the lake's fabled long-necked monster, may be a descendant of these reptiles.

STATE SONG

On May 22, 2000, Vermont officially adopted a new state song called
"These Green Mountains." The song was written by Diane B. Martin,
a native of Plainfield, Vermont.

THESE GREEN MOUNTAINS

Composed by Diane B. Martin; arranged by Rita Buglass Gluck

A VERMONT RECIPE

Vermont is the largest producer of maple syrup in the United States. Factories in Vermont bottle the syrup or use it in maple cream, maple sugar, taffy, salad dressing, and barbeque sauce. You can use maple syrup to make these cookies. Check the label of your maple syrup—chances are it's a product of Vermont!

MAPLE COOKIES

Ask an adult to help you with preheating the oven and with baking and removing the cookies.

1 cup butter
1 cup packed brown sugar
1 cup real maple syrup
1 egg
1 teaspoon vanilla extract

4 cups all-purpose flour
2 teaspoons baking soda
½ teaspoon salt
⅓ cup granulated sugar for decoration

1. Preheat the oven to 350° F. Grease cookie sheets, or spray thoroughly with non-stick cooking spray.

2. In large bowl, mix softened butter and brown sugar together until creamy. Add maple syrup, egg, and vanilla. Mix until well blended.

3. Sift the flour, baking soda, and salt together in separate bowl.

4. Add flour mixture by the cupful into other mixture until well blended.

5. Shape dough into 1-inch balls and roll in granulated sugar. Place on cookie sheets about 2 inches apart. Press dough balls until slightly flattened.

6. Bake 8 to 10 minutes. Remove to wire racks to cool completely. Makes about 36 cookies.

HISTORICAL TIMELINE

9000 B.C. Early peoples hunt in what later became Vermont.

A.D. 1300 Abenaki Indians settle in villages.

1609 Samuel de Champlain explores Abenaki homelands.

1666 Fort Sainte Anne is built by the French on an island in Lake Champlain.

1754 The French and Indian War (1754–1763) begins.

1763 The British take over the Champlain Valley at the end of the French and Indian War.

1764 The Green Mountain Boys, led by Ethan Allen, form to protect the Grants from the Yorkers.

1775 Ethan Allen captures Britian's Fort Ticonderoga.

1777 The Battle of Bennington is fought during the American Revolution; Vermont declares itself an independent government.

1783 The American Revolution ends, and the United States of America is formed.

1791 Vermont becomes the 14th state.

1865 Vermont's machine-tool industry is booming.

1910 Tourists begin flocking to Vermont.

1927 Floods on the Winooski and Connecticut Rivers kill Vermonters and destroy property.

1934 The state's first ski tow begins operating on a farm near Woodstock.

1939 World War II (1939–1945) begins, and 50,000 of Vermont's men and women serve in the armed forces.

1970 Laws are passed in Vermont to protect the environment.

1985 Madeleine Kunin becomes the first female governor of Vermont.

1991 Vermont celebrates 200 years of statehood.

1997 Act 60, a law that equalizes educational funding in Vermont, is passed.

2001 Vermont senator James Jeffords leaves the Republican Party and becomes an independent, giving the Democrats control of the U.S. Senate.

Calvin Coolidge

John Deere

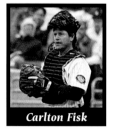
John Dewey

OUTSTANDING VERMONTERS

Chester A. Arthur (1829–1886) was the nation's 21st president. Vice president under James Garfield, Arthur became president in 1881 after Garfield was assassinated. He was born in Fairfield, Vermont.

Calvin Coolidge (1872–1933), born in Plymouth Notch, Vermont, became the 30th president of the United States after the death of President Warren G. Harding in 1923. Known as Silent Cal for his quiet manner, Coolidge led the nation during the 1920s.

John Deere (1804–1886) was a blacksmith who invented the first steel plow. His device made plowing easier and faster by turning heavy soil without getting clogged with dirt. By 1868 his firm, Deere and Company, was producing many types of farm machinery. Deere was born in Rutland, Vermont.

John Dewey (1859–1952) was an educator and philosopher from Burlington. He believed that students learn best by experimenting, instead of by memorizing facts. Dewey's ideas helped shape the nation's educational system.

Carlton Fisk (born 1947) was one of the greatest catchers in baseball history. After 11 seasons with the Boston Red Sox, Fisk moved to the Chicago White Sox in 1981. His major-league records include most games caught and most home runs hit by a catcher. Fisk was born in Bellows Falls, Vermont.

Carlton Fisk

Andrea Mead Lawrence (born 1932) began skiing in her backyard in Rutland, Vermont, at the age of four. In the 1952 Olympic Games, she became the first woman to win two gold medals in skiing. Lawrence earned her Olympic medals in the slalom and giant slalom events.

Andrea Mead Lawrence

George Perkins Marsh (1801–1882) wrote an influential book in 1864 called *Man and Nature*, which introduced the idea of conserving land and wildlife for future generations. He was born in Woodstock, Vermont.

Larkin Mead

Larkin Mead (1835–1910) was an artist who grew up in Brattleboro, Vermont. Mead sculpted a statue of Ethan Allen for Vermont's State House in 1861. He also created a statue of Allen for the U.S. Capitol building in Washington, D.C.

Clarina Nichols (1810–1885), a newspaper editor from West Townshend, Vermont, was an outspoken women's rights leader. In many articles, she argued that women should be able to inherit and own property as men could. Her efforts led government officials to pass laws granting women many new property rights in the 1800s.

Clarina Nichols

Elisha Graves Otis (1811–1861), from Halifax, Vermont, helped make elevators safe and popular. A master mechanic, Otis invented a safety device that could stop an elevator if its lifting rope broke.

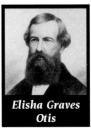

Elisha Graves Otis

Katherine Paterson

Katherine Paterson (born 1932) is a children's book author from Barre, Vermont, who has won two National Book Awards and two Newbery Medals. Among her best-known novels are *Bridge to Terabithia* and *Jacob Have I Loved*. Paterson's books have been published in 18 languages.

Patty Sheehan (born 1956) is a professional golfer. A member of the Ladies Professional Golf Association since 1980, Sheehan has won 35 victories in her career. In 1993 she was inducted into the LPGA Hall of Fame. Sheehan was born in Middlebury, Vermont.

Homer St. Francis

Joseph Smith (1805–1844), born in Sharon, Vermont, was the founder of the Mormon church—also called the Church of Jesus Christ of Latter-day Saints. In 1830 he published *The Book of Mormon*, which is the Mormons' holy book.

Homer St. Francis (born 1935), chief of the Abenaki nation, has worked for more than 30 years to reclaim Vermont for the Abenaki Indians, whose land was taken without a treaty. St. Francis also has preserved the Abenaki's hunting and fishing rights.

Alexander Twilight

Alexander Twilight (1795–1857) was born in Corinth, Vermont. After receiving a degree from Vermont's Middlebury College in 1823, Twilight became the country's first black college graduate. Elected to the Vermont legislature in 1836, he was the nation's first African American state legislator.

Rudy Vallee

Rudy Vallee (1901–1986), a singer and saxophonist, was born in Island Pond, Vermont. He is best known for crooning his theme song, "My Time Is Your Time," into a megaphone. In 1961 Vallee appeared in a play called *How to Succeed in Business Without Really Trying*.

Maria von Trapp (1905–1987) was a musician from Austria who moved with her family to Stowe, Vermont, in 1942. Her marriage to Baron Georg von Trapp and their family's escape from the Nazis was made famous in the movie *The Sound of Music*.

Maria von Trapp

Henry Wells (1805–1878) started the American Express Company, a delivery and banking company, along with William Fargo. As a founder of Wells, Fargo & Co., he helped settlers do business in the western United States. Both of Wells's companies grew into large financial institutions. Wells also founded a school for stutterers and a women's college. Wells was born in Thetford, Vermont.

Emma Hart Willard (1787–1870) established a girls' school at her home in Middlebury, Vermont, in 1814. She taught girls science, philosophy, and other subjects that were usually taught only to men. Willard later founded the Troy Female Seminary, which prepared women to be teachers.

Emma Hart Willard

William Griffith Wilson (1895–1971) of East Dorset, Vermont, established the self-help group Alcoholics Anonymous (AA). The Wilson House, the hotel once run by his mother and home of his birth, still holds AA meetings to help people with drinking problems.

Thomas Waterman Wood (1823–1903), a painter, created portraits of famous New Yorkers and painted scenes of African Americans during the Civil War. Born in Montpelier, Vermont, he founded the T. W. Wood Art Gallery in his hometown.

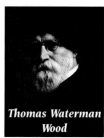

Thomas Waterman Wood

Brigham Young (1801–1877) became the leader of the Mormons in 1844. He led his followers to Utah, where they could practice their faith freely. Born in Whitingham, Vermont, Young founded Utah's first towns, factories, and schools.

Brigham Young

FACTS-AT-A-GLANCE

Nickname: Green Mountain State

Song: "These Green Mountains"

Motto: Freedom and Unity

Flower: red clover

Tree: sugar maple

Bird: hermit thrush

Animal: Morgan horse

Cold Water Fish: brook trout

Insect: honeybee

Mineral: talc

Date and ranking of statehood: March 4, 1791, the 14th state

Capital: Montpelier

Area: 9,249 square miles

Rank in area, nationwide: 43rd

Average January temperature: 17° F

Average July temperature: 68° F

Vermont's flag shows a tree, a cow, and bundles of grain, which are symbols of Vermont's agriculture.

POPULATION GROWTH

Thousands

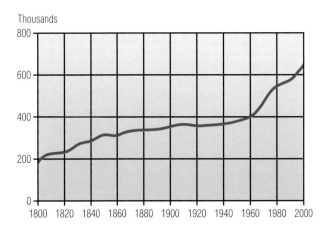

This chart shows how Vermont's population has grown from 1800 to 2000.

Vermont's seal, adopted in 1779, shows a pine tree with 14 branches, one branch for each of the original 13 states, plus Vermont. It also shows symbols that are important to Vermont's land and economy.

Population: 608,827 (2000 census)

Rank in population, nationwide: 49th

Major cities and populations: (2000 census) Burlington (38,889), Rutland (17,292), South Burlington (15,814), Barre (9,291), Montpelier (8,035), Saint Albans (7,650)

U.S. senators: 2

U.S. representatives: 1

Electoral votes: 3

Natural resources: forests, granite, gravel, limestone, marble, slate, talc

Agricultural products: apples, beef, butter, cattle, cheese, Christmas trees, eggs, hay, maple sugar, maple syrup, milk, potatoes, poultry, sheep

Manufactured goods: computers, flashlights, food products, lumber and wood products, machine tools, printed materials, teddy bears

WHERE VERMONTERS WORK

Services—63 percent (services includes jobs in trade; community, social and personal services; finance, insurance, and real estate; transportation, communication, and utilities)

Manufacturing—13 percent

Government—13 percent

Construction—7 percent

Agriculture—4 percent

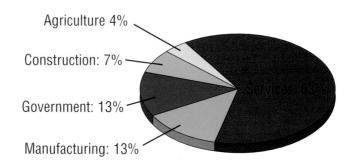

Agriculture 4%

Construction: 7%

Government: 13%

Manufacturing: 13%

Services: 63%

GROSS STATE PRODUCT

Services—63 percent

Manufacturing—18 percent

Government—12 percent

Construction—4 percent

Agriculture—3 percent

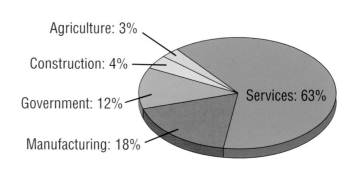

Agriculture: 3%

Construction: 4%

Government: 12%

Manufacturing: 18%

Services: 63%

VERMONT WILDLIFE

Mammals: beaver, black bear, bobcat, caribou, eastern red bat, lynx, mink, moose, muskrat, porcupine, rabbit, raccoon, red fox, skunk, squirrel, star-nosed mole, Virginia opossum, woodchuck

Birds: broad-winged hawk, golden eagle, great black-backed gull, red-throated loon, snowy owl, turkey vulture

Amphibians and reptiles: common mudpuppy, eastern newt, four-toed salamander, northern water snake, western striped chorus frog, wood turtle

Fish: Atlantic salmon, brook trout, lake sturgeon, northern pike, rainbow smelt, rainbow trout, yellow perch

Trees: American elm, ash, basswood, beech, birch, cedar, hemlock, poplar, red maple, spruce, sugar maple, white pine, white oak

Wild plants: anemone, arbutus, bloodwort, buttercup, coltsfoot, daisy, ferns, goldenrod, grasses, lilac, pussy willow, sedges, trout lily, violet, white trillium, yellow lady-slipper

Wild daisies grow near a Vermont lake.

PLACES TO VISIT

Appalachian Gap
> Located between Bristol and Waitsfield, this is one of Vermont's most scenic mountain passes.

Bennington Battle Monument, Bennington
> One of the tallest battle monuments in the world, the Bennington Battle Monument honors the colonists who defeated the British in the Battle of Bennington during the American Revolution in 1777.

President Calvin Coolidge State Historic Site, near Plymouth
> This landmark includes Coolidge's family home, where the former president took his oath of office. His grave is marked by a single gravestone in a nearby cemetery.

Ethan Allen Homestead, Burlington
> Visitors to Ethan Allen's last home can tour a visitors center and view exhibits dedicated to the leader of the Green Mountain Boys. Nature trails crisscross the grounds of the homestead.

Green Mountains National Forest
> In this forest in southern and central Vermont, hiking trails, parks, and recreation areas offer chances for outdoor activities. Fall foliage is spectacular.

Old Constitution House, Windsor

Vermont's first constitution was written in this two-story frame house. Built in 1772, the house was originally a tavern. It has been restored to the way it looked in the late 1700s, and it houses exhibits about Vermont's constitution.

Rock of Ages Granite Quarry, Barre

Visitors can watch granite blocks being quarried, sawed, polished, and carved here. The quarry, located in the Granite Capital of America, is one of the world's largest.

Shelburne Museum, Shelburne

This museum reconstructs aspects of early American life. It includes more than 30 historic buildings. Traditional New England toys, furniture, art, and more are on display. Visitors can explore an old lighthouse, a covered bridge, and the steamboat *Ticonderoga*.

Vermont Marble Exhibit, Proctor

Vermont boasts a long history of marble quarrying and finishing. This exhibit features the world's largest collection of various types of marble.

Vermont Teddy Bear Factory, Burlington

Teddy bear lovers of all ages can tour this factory to learn how the well-known company makes teddy bears by hand.

Bennington Battle Monument

ANNUAL EVENTS

Stowe Winter Carnival, Stowe—*January*

Vermont Maple Festival, Saint Albans—*April*

Kids' Fishing Derby, Brando—*May*

Kids' Maritime Festival, Ferrisburgh—*June*

Vermont Renaissance Festival—*June*

Hot Air Balloon Festival and Crafts Fair, Quechee—*June*

Vermont Quilt Festival, Northfield—*July*

Vermont Festival of the Arts, Mad River Valley—*August*

Championship Old-Time Fiddlers Contest, Bellows Falls—*August*

Apple Days Festival, Brattleboro—*September*

Pumpkin Lighting, Saint Albans—*October*

Fall Foliage Festival, Barre—*October*

LEARN MORE ABOUT VERMONT

BOOKS

General

Fradin, Dennis Brindell. *Vermont.* Danbury, CT: Children's Press, 1996.

Slayton, Tom, ed. *The Beauty of Vermont.* Montpelier, VT: Vermont Life Magazine, 1998. For older readers.

Thompson, Kathleen. *Vermont.* Orlando, FL: Raintree/Steck-Vaughn, 1996.

Special Interest

Arnosky, Jim. *Nearer Nature.* New York: Lothrop, Lee & Shepard, 1996. This book details aspects of country life on a small Vermont farm. For older readers.

Haas, Jessie. *Fire! My Parents' Story.* New York: Greenwillow, 1998. Tells the story of the author's parents' struggle with the aftermath of a fire that destroyed their Vermont farm.

Swinburne, Stephen S. *In Good Hands: Behind the Scenes at a Center for Orphaned and Injured Birds.* New York: Little, Brown & Company, 1998. At the Vermont Raptor Center, bird experts nurse orphaned or injured birds of prey and, if possible, release them into their natural habitat.

Fiction

Hurwitz, Johanna. *A Faraway Summer.* New York: William Morrow & Company, 1998. Set in 1910, this novel is about a young girl who leaves her crowded tenement in New York City to spend two weeks on a Vermont farm.

—————. *Yellow Blue Jay.* New York: Beech Tree Books, 1993. Eight-year-old Jay, who lives in the city, panics when his family announces that they'll be spending two weeks in the Vermont woods.

Lunn, Janet. *The Hollow Tree.* New York: Viking Children's Books, 2000. Set in 1777, this book follows the adventures of a young girl who unknowingly becomes an undercover spy for the British.

Peck, Robert Newton. *A Day No Pigs Would Die.* New York: Random House Children's Publishing, 1973. A classic novel about a young Vermont farm boy who is the only surviving son of a dying father.

WEBSITES

State of Vermont Home Page
<http://www.state.vt.us>
The official website of the state of Vermont features information on its government, the University of Vermont, and the state libraries.

Vermont Life Explorer Page
<http://www.1-800-vermont.com >
The official site of the Vermont Department of Tourism and Marketing provides information about events, things to do, and places to stay.

Burlington Free Press
<http://www.burlingtonfreepress.com/>
Burlington's newspaper provides national and local news for Vermonters.

Vermont Secretary of State Office Kids Home Page
<http://www.sec.state.vt.us/KidsPage/homepage.htm>
This site provides fun and informative facts about Vermont's government, geography, history, and attractions, plus a quiz and pictures for kids to print out and color.

PRONUNCIATION GUIDE

Abenaki (a-buh-NAH-kee)

Barre (BA-ree)

Brattleboro (BRAT-uhl-buhr-oh)

Champlain (sham-PLAYN)

Connecticut (kuh-NEHD-uh-kuht)

Iroquois (IHR-uh-kwoy)

Montpelier (mahnt-PEEL-yuhr)

Petoubouque (BIHT-uh-bahk)

Taconic (tuh-KAWN-ihk)

Ticonderoga (ty-kahn-duhr-OH-guh)

Winooski (wuh-NOO-skee)

GLOSSARY

colony: a territory ruled by a country some distance away

constitution: the system of basic laws or rules of a government, society, or organization; the document in which these laws or rules are written

erosion: the wearing away of the earth's surface by the forces of water, wind, or ice

glacier: a large body of ice and snow that moves slowly over land

immigrant: a person who moves into a foreign country and settles there

Latino: a person living in the United States who either came from or has ancestors from Latin America. Latin America includes Mexico and most of Central and South America.

missionary: a person sent out by a religious group to spread its beliefs to other people

precipitation: rain, snow, and other forms of moisture that fall to earth

quarry: an open pit dug by miners for obtaining limestone, marble, slate, granite, or other building stone

INDEX

PHOTO ACKNOWLEDGMENTS

© Michael T. Sedam/CORBIS, p. front cover (left); © Phil Schermeister/CORBIS, p. front cover (right); James P. Blair/CORBIS, pp. 2-3, 48; © Lee Snider; Lee Snider/CORBIS, pp. 3, 24; Digital Cartographics, pp. 1, 8, 9, 49; Janda Thompson, pp. 4, 7, 17, 39, 53; Erwin C. "Bud" Nielsen, Tucson, AZ, p. 6; Jerry Hennen, pp. 7, 11, 14; Carolyn Bates, pp. 10, 15, 50; Vermont Department of Travel and Tourism, pp. 12, 13, 16, 73; Mae Scanlan, p. 17; Special Collections, University of Vermont Library, pp. 18, 19, 20; Library of Congress, pp. 22, 25, 66 (top), 67 (second from bottom); The American Revolution, Dover Publications, p. 26; © Adam Woolfitt/CORBIS; p. 28; Vermont Historical Society, pp. 30, 31, 32, 35; Brattleboro Photos, Inc., p. 34; © Thomas P. Benincas, Jr., pp. 36, 44, 55; Russell Vermontiana Collection, p. 37; © Craig Aurness/CORBIS, p. 39; © Gerry Lemmo, pp. 40, 43, 54, 57; NE Stock Photo: Effin Older, pp. 41, 46; Margo Taussig Pinkerton, p 42; Art Phaneuf, p. 47; © Roman Soumar/CORBIS, p. 45; Betty Groskin, p. 51; © Buddy Mays/CORBIS, p. 52; © Mary Ann McDonald/CORBIS, p. 56; © David Muench/CORBIS, p. 58; © Jane P. Downton/Root Resources, p. 60; Jack Lindstrom, p. 61; Tim Seeley, pp. 63, 71-72; Deere & Company, p. 66 (second from top); Dictionary of American Portraits, pp. 66 (second from bottom), 67 (second from top), 69 (second from top); Chicago White Sox, p. 66 (bottom); UPI/Bettmann, p. 67 (top); © Bettmann/CORBIS, pp. 67 (bottom), 69 (bottom); Jill Paton Walsh, p. 68 (top); The Sovereign Abenaki Nation, p. 68 (second from top); Orleans County (VT) Historical Society, p. 68 (second from bottom); Hollywood Book and Poster Company, p. 68 (bottom); Frank L. Forward/Trapp Family Lodge, p. 69 (top); T. W. Wood Art Gallery, Montpelier, VT, p. 69 (second from bottom); Jean Matheny, p. 70 (top); Minneapolis Public Library, p. 75; © Jan Reynolds/CORBIS, p. 80.

The revised **Hello U.S.A.** series takes you on a tour of the history, geography, people, economy, and environment of the 50 states, plus Puerto Rico and Washington, D.C. Colorful photos, easy-to-read text, and fascinating sidebars provide the facts you need for research, reports, or even a cross-country trip. So pack your bags and get ready to say **Hello U.S.A.!**

NEW FEATURES INCLUDE:

- ★ Completely up-to-date information, including 2000 U.S. census data
- ★ New maps, charts, and graphs
- ★ New lists of related books and websites
- ★ Expanded Places to Visit section
- ★ State wildlife, state song, and recipe

First Avenue Editions
An imprint of
Lerner Publishing Group

ISBN 0-8225-4135-1

50695

9 780822 541356